ST. PATRICK'S
Cathedral

- ÉDITIONS DU SIGNE -

Photo Credit: Peter Mauss/Esto

ÉDITIONS
DU SIGNE

Publisher:
Éditions du Signe
1, rue Alfred Kastler - Eckbolsheim
B.P. 94 – 67038 Strasbourg, Cedex 2, France
Tel: 011 333 88 78 91 91
Fax: 011 333 88 78 91 99
www.editionsdusigne.fr
email: info@editionsdusigne.fr

Publishing director: Christian Riehl
Director of publication: Joëlle Bernhard

Author: Thomas G. Young
Publishing consultant: Patrick Danczewski

Layout: Éditions du Signe - Anthony Kinné - 108058
Cover pictures: Front/Back. Photo credit: John Glover

Photo Credit: John Glover

TABLE of Contents

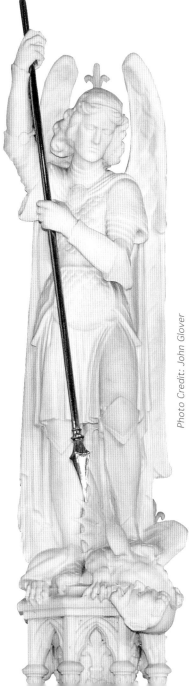

Photo Credit: John Glover

"A House of God for all people." "America's Parish Church."

These are titles given to St. Patrick's by none other than His Holiness Pope Benedict XVI and by His Excellency, Archbishop Timothy Dolan. Our Holy Father and our Archbishop recognize the uniqueness of this magnificent Gothic Jewel in the heart of Manhattan. We welcome you, our readers, to experience this urban treasure through this newest book about the Cathedral.

For over 130 years pilgrims have come to worship the Lord, to find peace for their souls or just to get a respite from the hustle and bustle of Fifth Avenue. For people of all religions, St. Patrick's is a special place. Even people of no religion see the beauty and serenity of a unique New York City landmark.

A number of years ago, a book was published detailing the windows of the Cathedral. This volume is in continuity with that earlier volume yet also describes important features inside and out of our beautiful Church. This current volume is a reminder and an invitation. If you have been one of the millions of visitors who pass through our bronze doors each year, this volume is a reminder of the sights and sounds you experienced here. If you have not visited us yet, this volume is an invitation to come and see what others have seen and to experience the uniqueness of St. Patrick's Cathedral.

An expanded title of St. Patrick's would identify it as the "Metropolitan Cathedral of the Archdiocese of New York." We are the place where the seat of the Archbishop is located and this "seat" is the symbol of the teaching authority of our Archbishop. We are grateful to Mr. Thomas G. Young for this expansive description of the historical context of the Archdiocese of New York in which the Cathedral is placed and for his encyclopedic knowledge of the sum of the parts which together make up St. Patrick's. We are also grateful to Monsignor Thomas Shelley, American Catholic historian, for his invaluable contribution. More than most Churches of any importance, the Cathedral is filled with statues, altars, shrines and other details. We are grateful to the photographers who brought light and life to these items of stone, glass, paint and marble.

This volume would not have been possible without the planning of Mr. Patrick Danczewski, the Director of our Gift Shops and the staff of Editions du Signe. We owe them a debt of gratitude for their inspiration and dedication to the production of this volume. Finally, a hundred thousand thank you's to our ancestors in the faith who built and maintained this testimony to the presence of God in the midst of the city.

So, in the name of all who are associated with this wonderful Cathedral, I invite you to experience and to love what we all call OUR Cathedral of St. Patrick.

Msgr. Robert T. Ritchie
Rector

HISTORY
OF THE ARCHDIOCESE
OF *New York*

PUBLIC BUILDINGS IN THE CITY OF NEW-YORK.
Drawn by A. J. Davis—Engraved by J. Eddy
FOR THE NEW-YORK MIRROR.

• Public buildings in the city of New York, 1830. Old St. Patrick's Cathedral is on the top right.
Photo Credit: Picture Collection, The New York Public Library, Astor, Lenox and Tilden Foundations.

Before 1808, the Diocese of Baltimore was the only diocese in the United States. The New York Diocese, with only two churches in all of New York State and much of New Jersey (the territory of the New York Diocese), was created that year together with three other new dioceses. Its first bishop, Richard Luke Concanen, stationed in Rome, never spent a single day in his diocese due to travel problems created by the Napoleonic wars. An absent bishop was only one of many seemingly insurmountable problems New York faced such as lack of clergy, inadequate financing and scanty numbers of practicing Catholics. In fact practicing or non-practicing Catholics were something of a rarity in an essentially Protestant country where many Americans looked askance at members of a "popish" Church whom they disdained.

But the Catholic population increased rapidly during the first few decades of the 19th Century, especially Irish Catholic immigrants, many of whom arrived to provide the labor force for building the Erie Canal to open a water route from the Atlantic Ocean to the Great Lakes. Thus, from its earliest days and continuing well into the 20th Century, Irish Catholics provided a core group of Catholic faithful in New York. Bishop Concanen's successors during the first half of the century, Bishop John Connolly and Bishop John Dubois, struggled heroically to shepherd their flocks (the numbers increasing by 1840 to 75,000 souls from a mere 200 in 1785), traveling across primitive roads using primitive means of transport with few priests to minister in widely scattered churches. Not surprisingly, anti-Catholic bigotry grew in the 1830s and 1840s, often fueled by "nativisits" who deeply resented the arrival of so many foreigners - and especially Catholic foreigners - to American shores. Despite the difficulties, or perhaps because of them, New York already produced figures of outstanding saintliness such as St. Elizabeth Ann Seton, foundress of the Sisters of Charity; St. John Neumann, later Bishop of Philadelphia; and Venerable Pierre Toussaint, a former slave whose exemplary charitable works spread his fame.

• *Bishop John Connolly, O.P.*
(1814-1825).
Photo Credit: Chris Sheridan

Early in the 1840s, Bishop John Hughes became New York's fourth chief shepherd and almost immediately rose to a position of America's most famous Catholic church leader. Determined to win for Catholics a place in American society on an equal plane with all other citizens, the steely fighter went on the attack against any he perceived to be enemies of his Church or his people. He fought - and won - battles against some Catholics (trustees of churches) who he felt usurped his authority, either temporal or spiritual. When he learned of anti-Catholic prejudice in the public schools, he waged war against political leaders to correct the inequity, eventually inaugurating a system of Catholic schools. And when nativists threatened to spread anti-Catholic rioting from Philadelphia to New York, he faced them down asserting that he would defend Catholic churches even if New York would "become a second Moscow" (referring to that city's destruction when invaded by Napoleon). Bishop Hughes may have been both the most admired and at the same time the most detested man in New York, and perhaps far beyond its borders.

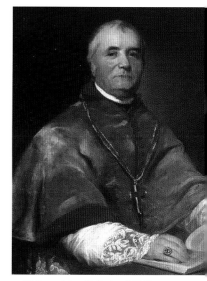

• *Bishop John Dubois, P.S.S.*
(1826-1842)
Photo Credit: Chris Sheridan

By 1850, following the deluge of immigrants into the City resulting from the Irish potato famine, the Catholic population exploded. New dioceses in Albany and Buffalo were carved out of the New York Diocese in 1847 and in July of 1850 New York was made an Archdiocese with Hughes appointed the first Archbishop. So great was the increase in population that in 1853 two more dioceses were established (Brooklyn and Newark) from territory within the Archdiocese. The Archbishop proclaimed that it was time for New York to have a great Cathedral on the scale of those of Europe, and plans

• *Archbishop John Joseph Hughes*
(1842-1864).
Photo Credit: Chris Sheridan

• Imposing the Cardinal's Berretta: Upon His Grace Archbishop McCloskey of New York, by His Grace Archbishop Bayley of Baltimore, at St. Patricks Cathedral, N.Y. April 27th, 1875. Photo Credit: Museum of the city of New York

for the present St. Patrick's Cathedral rapidly took shape. By 1859 there were scores of new churches in the Archdiocese. During the Civil War, the Archbishop served as an emissary of President Lincoln to persuade France to support the Union. During the draft riots in New York, the worst in American history up to that point, he attempted to calm the storms by pleading with Catholics to help end violence and destruction, despite his rapidly failing health. When he died in 1864, in addition to the scores of new churches, 75% of the parishes had schools, there were institutions for the care of orphans, two colleges, some private academies, vocational training schools and a seminary, all staffed by many of the religious congregations he had brought to New York.

John McCloskey, Bishop of Albany, New York, became New York's next Archbishop. The era following the Civil War was one of growth and development for the City, and many immigrants moved into the mainstream of society. A few accumulated great wealth, although not on the scale of such industrial titans as Vanderbilt or Morgan, while most Catholics worked to lift themselves out of earlier impoverished conditions and provide decent livelihoods for their families. New York's Democratic Party provided a stepping stone into middle class life through politics as many Irish Catholics immersed themselves in the process. And as the City grew, so did the Church. Recognizing the central role New York had assumed in American life, Rome conferred the special honor of a "red hat" on Archbishop McCloskey, making

• John Cardinal McCloskey (1864-1885). Photo Credit: Chris Sheridan

him the first American cardinal, indeed, the first in the Western Hemisphere. In 1879 the Cardinal opened the new St. Patrick's Cathedral, America's largest and grandest church at that time. (St. Patrick's is no longer the largest church in the country). By the time of his death in 1885, there were 600,000 Catholics in the Archdiocese served by over 400 priests and 2300 nuns and religious brothers in 230 churches and many orphanages, industrial training schools and hospitals.

When Michael Corrigan succeeded Cardinal McCloskey as Archbishop, New York was the largest archdiocese in the country. And it continued to grow at a hectic pace. By 1900 Archbishop Corrigan had opened an additional 250 institutions (churches, schools, convents, rectories, etc.) in just the previous ten years. These no longer served only the Irish, since immigrants now arrived from many European countries, especially Jews escaping persecution in their homelands. Among the Catholics were a great number of Italians and Germans, and to a lesser extent, Poles and others from northern and eastern Europe. Providing spiritual care to these new arrivals was of paramount importance. The Archbishop was most proud of the erection of the country's possibly most famous seminary, St. Joseph's, in the Dunwoodie section of Yonkers, New York. By the end of the 20th Century, over 2200 priests would receive their training in this institution.

Archbishop, later Cardinal, John Farley began his episcopate in 1902 when there were 1,200,000 Catholics in the Archdiocese. By the time of his death in 1918, the number had risen at a slower pace than earlier to 1,325,000, as large numbers of Catholics moved into the middle class and left the crowded city for the suburbs, many outside the confines of the Archdiocese. Within its territory, however, the Bronx, Staten Island and Westchester showed remarkable growth during these decades. And so it was in these counties that new Catholic buildings appeared most often. But during the Cardinal's final years the world was involved in the worst war it had ever experienced to that time. America entered World War I in 1917 and New York quickly responded to the need for military chaplains sending 87 priests to serve. The most famous was Father Francis P. Duffy, chaplain of the "fighting 69th" Regiment, respected by his men for his bravery and dedication to their welfare. New York Catholics at home supported the soldiers with the most generous contributions of any diocese in the country during the 1918 fundraising drive.

• *Archbishop Michael Augustine Corrigan (1885-1902).*
Photo Credit: Chris Sheridan

• *John Murphy Cardinal Farley (1902-1918).*
Photo Credit: Chris Sheridan

Patrick Cardinal Hayes led the New York Catholic community from 1919 until 1938. Al Smith, the first Catholic to run for President of the United States, was born and raised in the City. During the last half of the Cardinal's term the nation suffered through the Great Depression. A quarter of the people were unemployed in the City. The population of the Archdiocese actually declined during this period to about 1,000,000. There were more poor Catholics in New York at this time than anywhere in the United States and the Cardinal's charitable efforts in his see under a new agency called Catholic Charities of the Archdiocese caused him to be seen as the "Cardinal of Charities." Dorothy Day's Catholic Worker Movement was begun during the depression within the confines of the Archdiocese. During the war, Cardinal (then bishop) Hayes had been in charge of the Military Ordinariate as auxiliary bishop of New York. When he became Archbishop of New York, the military remained under his jurisdiction, and would continue its New York association until the 1980s.

One of the best-known of America's prelates, Francis Spellman, became Archbishop of New York in 1939. His tenure was longer than any New York archbishop's before or after him. Like Cardinal Hayes, he was Military Vicar for the Armed Forces, a position which brought him worldwide exposure, first during World War II and later during the Korean War, since he spent long periods attending to his military charges all over the world in addition to his Archdiocesan flock. It also afforded him close contact with political figures worldwide and especially in the United States. At home, his building campaign, especially a large number of educational institutions, was the last major expansion of physical facilities in the history of the Archdiocese. The enrollment in elementary and secondary Catholic schools almost doubled by the mid-1960s, and it was estimated that, except for the public school systems of New York City and Chicago, the school systems of the Archdiocese of New York and the Diocese of Brooklyn together had the largest enrollment of students in the country.

It was during the Spellman years that a new migration into the Archdiocese took place, this time, not from Europe, but from Puerto Rico. The Cardinal determined to address the pastoral challenge by sending large numbers of priests to Puerto Rico to study Spanish, so that by the mid-1960s there were over 200 Spanish-speaking priests throughout the Archdiocese, especially in Manhattan and the Bronx. One of the auxiliary bishops serving under Cardinal Spellman was Fulton Sheen, one of the most popular preachers in American history, resulting from his widely-popular radio and television programs. But, also, the Cardinal's prominence challenged the fame of such earlier figures as Bishop Hughes and Cardinal Gibbons.

Towards the end of his life, the Second Vatican Council was convoked in Rome. After its conclusion, Cardinal Spellman felt some liturgical changes were moving too quickly, but before his death he implemented many of the conciliar directives. And one of the last major events of his long tenure, and certainly one of the joys of his life, was arranging the visit of Pope Paul VI to New York, the first visit of any Pope to America. The joy of that occasion was tempered by the difficulties surrounding the Vietnam War, difficulties which took a toll on his health. He died before the war ended and before turmoil in the Church after the Vatican Council had subsided.

That turmoil would be borne heavily by the next Archbishop, Terence Cardinal Cooke, whose term began on the same day Dr. Martin Luther King was assassinated in 1968. Two months later he officiated at the funeral of New York Senator Robert Kennedy. These events portended further sorrows to envelope both the country and the church during the next fifteen years of Cardinal Cooke's time as New York's Catholic leader. The Archdiocese, like the Church throughout the country, experienced a sharp decline in numbers of practicing Catholics, resignations from the priesthood and religious life causing great shortages in pastoral care, and a disintegration of Church authority in the eyes of many. At the same time, civil disturbances raged through New York, especially in the South Bronx where crime, arson and general deterioration were often the norm. It was the Catholic churches which served as the only oases in the midst of such terrible suffering until the 1980s when very slow recovery began to ensue. But the Cardinal's management skills kept the parishes functioning, especially the schools despite declining enrollments.

• *Terence James Cardinal Cooke (1968-1983).*
Photo Credit: Chris Sheridan

In 1979, four years before his death, Cardinal Cooke was host to Pope John Paul II on the second visit of a reigning pope to New York. The joy apparent in the Cardinal's demeanor masked his suffering due to a cancer he carried for several years before his death. His reputation for holiness was evident in the huge numbers of mourners who filed past his casket in October 1983. Over 900 priests attended his funeral Mass.

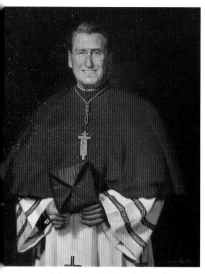

• *John Joseph Cardinal O'Connor (1984-2000).*
Photo Credit: Chris Sheridan

A very different style of leadership characterized the years when John Cardinal O'Connor was Archbishop of New York beginning in 1984. His public appearances, especially in the pulpit of St. Patrick's Cathedral and at frequent news conferences and television appearances, made him one of the highest profile Catholic leaders in the country. His proclamation of Catholic moral teaching often resulted in large protests, especially by members of the homosexual community, even though the Archdiocese did more than any other organization to help AIDS patients. Social programs grew during the O'Connor years and the number of Catholics increased to over 2,300,000 by 1998. Despite the financial burden of supporting schools with few religious nuns and brothers in poor neighborhoods with fewer students, the Cardinal was determined to keep the schools functioning. His support for life at all stages led him to found a new religious community of nuns, the Sisters of Life, which grew in numbers rapidly. He served as host for Pope John Paul II during the pontiff's second visit to New York in 1995. Like his predecessor, at the end Cardinal O'Connor suffered from cancer which ultimately claimed his life in May 2000.

The same month, Edward Cardinal Egan began his tenure as Archbishop of New York. The serious financial difficulties faced by the Archdiocese were in expert hands to set the Church's finances on a firm foundation by a realignment of the churches, schools, hospitals and other institutions under his care. Early in his administration, the horror of the September 11, 2001 attack on New York's World Trade Center brought his spiritual leadership to the forefront. For months after the tragedy he led the Church in giving comfort and support to the thousands of families torn apart by death and injury, as funeral Masses and other services followed one upon another. As time and constant prayers slowly began the healing, Cardinal Egan visited every corner of the huge Archdiocese, now grown to 2,500,000 souls, bringing pastoral care to his flock over the next several years.

• *Edward Michael Cardinal Egan (2000-2009).*
Photo Credit: Chris Sheridan

He succeeded in raising funds to support Catholic education for many unable to afford tuition costs while beginning construction of new churches in outer counties for the first time in many years as demographic changes required. The great joy of celebrating the 200th anniversary of the Archdiocese of New York was spread to its borders with many liturgies and events throughout an entire year so that as many Catholics as possible could take part. Certainly the zenith of the celebrations came with the visit to New York of Pope Benedict XVI in 2008, with Cardinal Egan at his side at each event.

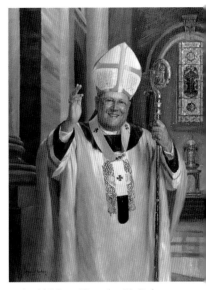

The present Archbishop of New York, Timothy M. Dolan, was installed in April 2009 after serving as Archbishop of Milwaukee since 2002. His priestly ministry began in the Archdiocese of St. Louis and continued in that archdiocese as well as in Washington, D. C. where he was Secretary for the Apostolic Nunciature, and in Rome where he was Rector of the Pontifical North American College. He was an auxiliary bishop in St. Louis before his appointment to Milwaukee. In the short time he has been in New York, he has energetically engaged in pastoral visits throughout the Archdiocese and in numerous civic and religious events in the City.

• *Archbishop Timothy M. Dolan (2009-present).*
Official portrait painted by Patrice Hudson

Photo Credit: Chris Sheridan

• *St. Patrick's Cathedral.*
Photo taken from St. Patrick's Cathedral Archives

HISTORY
OF THE *Cathedral*

The present St. Patrick's Cathedral is not New York's first. In 1808, the same year the Diocese of New York was created, plans were made for the new bishop's church, named St. Patrick's Cathedral, and located in the lower part of Manhattan in a section even then outside the center of everyday life. When it opened in 1815 it was the largest church in the City. When New York became an archdiocese, Archbishop Hughes proposed to build a structure which he considered more suitable for a growing city and one "worthy of our increasing numbers, intelligence and wealth as a religious community." James Renwick, one of the finest American architects of the 19th Century, was chosen in 1853 to design it, and the cornerstone was laid in 1858 during a ceremony attended by an estimated 100,000 citizens. Work progressed slowly until funds were exhausted in 1860, and the Civil War delayed further work until Archbishop (later Cardinal) McCloskey resumed construction in 1865. By 1879 it was ready to open, although Renwick's design was modified considerably by lack of funds, so that a central tower, a chevet with radiating chapels at the east end, massive flying buttresses and a masonry ceiling were eliminated.

A smaller addition of a Lady Chapel and two adjacent chapels came years later, but the stone ceiling, flying buttresses and central tower were never built.

The spires were added between 1885 and 1888, and the Lady Chapel addition followed at the turn of the 20th Century, designed by another prominent architect, Charles Mathews. At the same time, sacristies were added below the new chapels and a crypt below the sanctuary. The reason the addition was smaller than Renwick's proposal was because the residence of the Archbishop at 50th Street and Madison Avenue and the rectory at 51st Street required some of the land.

Inside the building, altars were installed in the nave chapels during the tenure of Archbishop Michael Corrigan in the 1890s, and most of the statues in the transepts were carved at the same time, as were the magnificent stations of the cross. The stained glass windows at the lower level and around the apse were in place when the Cathedral opened, but the frames of the other windows contained a clearer glass until gradually each received stained glass over a period of many decades in the 20th Century. The original organ was in a gallery where the present grand organ is, but was neither large nor of great power. The original high altar was backed by a massive reredos (screen) rising fifty feet and set almost at the rear wall. The floor was wood covered by carpet over which were box pews.

• *Interior view of Old
St. Patrick's Cathedral,
New York, 1853.*
*Photo Credit:
Picture Collection, The New York
Public Library, Astor, Lenox
and Tilden Foundations*

The sanctuary was smaller than the present space by one bay (space from one pillar to the next), so that pew seating capacity was larger than it is today. The nineteen bells in the north tower arrived in the late 1890s.

The first rector of the Cathedral (although the Archbishop is the pastor, the rector administers the church) was Msgr. William Quinn who served from 1879 until his death in 1886. His successor, Msgr. Michael Lavelle, was at St. Patrick's his entire priestly life and was rector for over fifty years. Regular services, which began immediately after the dedication ceremony in May 1879, were enhanced by two choirs, an adult choir of sixty voices and a fifty-voice boys choir. Parishioners ranged from the very poor, to hard-working laborers to the very wealthy, many of whom built homes on or near what was becoming the most fashionable street in the City, Fifth Avenue. In the immediate neighborhood of the Cathedral were Catholic orphan asylums, a college, a fashionable hotel and mansions of business barons like the Vanderbilts. In the late 19th Century, visitors from around the world were already attracted to what was recognized as the finest church building in America.

• Fair held in the Cathedral six months before opening. Each Parish booth helped to furnish the interior.
Photo Credit: Museum of the city of New York

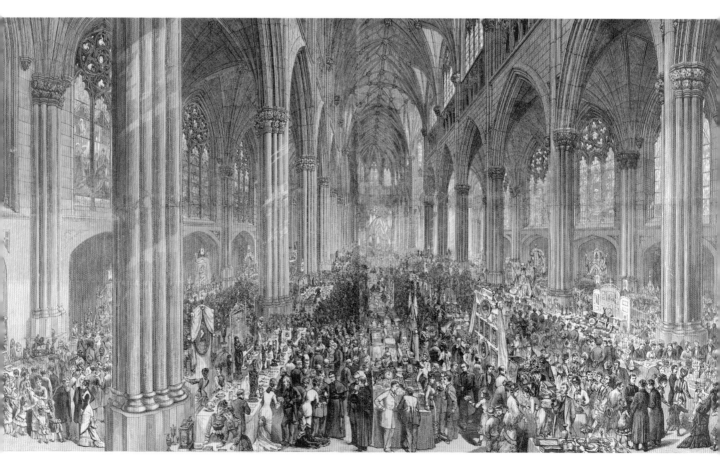

Cardinal Farley was Archbishop in the early years of the 20th Century, a time when Catholics in New York were growing in number and importance. The Cathedral was invariably the center of religious liturgies and special ceremonies like the 1908 centennial of the Archdiocese, and the 1910 consecration of the building held after all its debts were eliminated. When parades passed on Fifth Avenue, a large reviewing stand for dignitaries covered the 5th Avenue steps. During these years, improvements were made both inside and

• *1906 photograph of Easter Sunday in front of St. Patrick's. Photo Credit:*
Museum of the city of New York

outside such as new terraces and steps around the building and new altars inside. The beautiful Pieta statue arrived in 1915. During America's participation in World War I, there were many Masses for fallen sons of St. Patrick's. In 1918 after the death of Cardinal Farley, lines of the faithful waiting to view his remains stretched along Fifth and Madison Avenues as far as 70th Street.

One of America's finest musicians, the organist Pietro Yon, took the reins of the music program at St. Patrick's in the next decade when Patrick Cardinal Hayes was Archbishop. Yon's reputation - like St. Patrick's - was international in scope, and he counted luminaries in the arts among his friends. At the end of the 1920s Fulton J. Sheen, "the outstanding preacher in the history of the Church in America," began his association with St. Patrick's. It continued for the next half-century. During these prosperous years, a complete renovation of the Cathedral was planned under the able direction of Msgr. Lavelle, and much of it was carried out until the Depression of the 1930s abruptly interrupted it. But before the effects of the economic tragedy took hold, the Cathedral assumed an entirely different appearance. The sanctuary was expanded into the transept, raised several feet from the pavement and surrounded by an intricately carved oak screen; European stained glass filled the windows of the Lady Chapel; the organ gallery was rebuilt for one of the finest organs in the country; a second organ was erected near the chancel; a new altar railing was set in place; a new baptistry was installed; new lights illuminated the building; and the entire floor was paved with marble supporting new pews.

• *1906 photograph of Easter Sunday in front of St. Patrick's. Photo Credit:*
Museum of the city of New York

• St. Patrick's Cathedral view from Madison Avenue early 20th Century.
Photo Credit: Photography Collection, Miriam and Ira D. Wallach Division of Art,
Prints and Photographs, The New York Public Library, Astor, Lenox and Tilden Foundations.

In the subsequent difficult years, reduced revenue assisted the poor and suffering as much as possible. Absent any government aid programs at that time, poor widows were employed by Msgr. Lavelle for many tasks, those employed were instructed of their moral duty to assist the unemployed, special collections were taken for the poor and volunteers passed from door to door in the parish collecting funds for the needy. In their time of trouble the faithful thronged to pray in the largest numbers in the Cathedral's history. But the gloom of the era was lifted on occasions such as when Eugenio Cardinal Pacelli, later Pope Pius XII, visited, or on special feast days when Pietro Yon's skill over the organ manuals produced sounds unheard anywhere else unless it was at his Carnegie Hall concerts, or when great figures from the world of politics, sports or entertainment shared the pews with "ordinary" Catholics, or when the spellbinding preacher, Msgr. Fulton J. Sheen, mounted the steps of the pulpit to encourage the faithful.

Cardinal Hayes died almost as the Great Depression neared its end. But its end was largely brought about by a worse tragedy, the start of the most costly war ever. Francis J. Spellman was appointed Archbishop in 1939, shortly before World War II's hostilities began in Europe. England's need for war supplies from America put many to work in the two years before America entered the war. Also in 1939, St. Patrick's famous rector, Msgr. Michael Lavelle, died, succeeded by Bishop Joseph Flannelly. The new archbishop soon decided to complete the renovation work begun a decade earlier and in 1941 the Lady Chapel received a new altar while design work proceeded on replacement of the main altar. Two years later the magnificent bronze baldachin (canopy) over a new high altar appeared with an open view beyond it to the east end of the Lady Chapel. A new statue of St. Patrick was added near the *cathedra* (Archbishop's chair) and magnificent new windows spanned the upper levels of the transept and over the sanctuary. During the war, the Cathedral opened a canteen for visiting servicemen, and service flags were suspended both inside and outside the Cathedral recording the number of Catholics in the Archdiocese serving their country. At the beginning of 1944, the banners recorded almost 150,000 men and women in service and almost 1400 gold stars were a grim reminder of New York Catholics who had given their lives. Pietro Yon died in 1943 and Charles Courboin became the new music director.

• *St. Patrick's Cathedral during the construction of Rockefeller Center, c. 1933-1934*
Photo Credit:
Museum of the city of New York

After the war, blasting for construction in the neighborhood caused a loosening of some masonry and the consequent need for a complete restoration of the facade. When it was completed three

• *St. Patrick's on Easter Sunday 1941.*
Photo Credit:
Museum of the city of New York

years later, some of the intricate stone carvings were gone including the gargoyles on the Lady Chapel, open niches intended for statuary were filled with marble, the wooden roof supports were replaced with steel and there were new marble entrances around the doors. The great rose window was filled with beautiful stained glass, and shortly afterwards, the wooden doors at the 5th Avenue entrances were replaced by bronze doors.

The decade of the 1940s brought many prominent visitors to the Cathedral including Winston Churchill, the former King Edward VIII of England and presidents of several countries. Liturgies included the funeral Masses for Ignace Jan Paderewski, famous pianist and former president of Poland, and Babe Ruth. Regular parishioners included Al Smith and James A. Farley.

During the 1950s, although Cardinal Spellman was often traveling throughout the world visiting troops who were fighting the

Korean War, at St. Patrick's great crowds flocked to liturgies. Communion breakfasts flourished, special Masses were offered in various non-Latin rites liturgies, and weddings, funerals and other special liturgies were so numerous that a Cathedral chapel was opened near the northern limits of the parish. Guest choirs from distant places sang frequently, and the Cathedral choirs made recordings. The last unfilled windows at the upper levels received stained glass and the bells in the north tower were electrified during these years.

During the Vietnam War of the 1960s Cardinal Spellman once again often was away from the Cathedral visiting American troops. Changes both in the life of the Church and in civil life greatly affected St. Patrick's during the tumultuous decade of the 1960s. The vernacular Mass was introduced in New York before it began in many other dioceses. There were demonstrations for and against America's involvement in the Vietnam War, some even inside the Cathedral. Conversely, one of the happiest events in American Catholic history occurred when the first ever papal visit to America brought Pope Paul VI to St. Patrick's in 1965. This highlight of Cardinal Spellman's life came shortly before his death in 1967.

The next Archbishop of New York, Terence Cardinal Cooke, is remembered as a saintly priest. His cause for canonization was introduced shortly after his death in 1983. After his installation, he appointed Msgr. James F. Rigney as rector of the Cathedral. During the Cardinal's episcopate St. Patrick's was the site of many "firsts" such as musical concerts by leading orchestras, conductors, soloists and choirs including the Metropolitan Opera Orchestra, Leopold Stokowski, Zubin Mehta, Luciano Pavarotti, Placido Domingo and the Vienna Boys Choir. Under Msgr. Rigney's leadership, frequent ecumenical services took place in the Cathedral, prominent figures in the fields of government, sports and entertainment attended services and the numbers of visitors from around the world soared to their highest levels in history. A program of hundreds of volunteers was instituted in 1975, as was a program to address the needs of elderly neighbors and a program for young adults. The entire interior was restored to its pristine beauty early in the l970s and at the end of the decade the exterior facade was made to sparkle. John Grady, the new music director, brought famous artists from all corners of the globe to enrich the liturgy or to perform religious pieces for large crowds.

• *St. Elizabeth Ann Seton's shrine.*
Photo Credit: John Glover

THE HUNDREDTH YEAR

• *100th anniversary logo.*
Taken from Saint Patrick's
Cathedral Archives

New shrines were added to honor the American saints Elizabeth Seton and John Neumann, and fine artistic statuary was added to honor St. Anthony, Sts. Peter and Paul and St. Jude. As was the case in 1965, a papal visit to St. Patrick's, this time by Pope John Paul II, was a highlight of these years during the pope's two day visit in October 1979. That same year, St. Patrick's celebrated its 100th birthday culminating in a grand Mass in May following a year of special events. At the end of the year, Archbishop Fulton J. Sheen, so much a part of St. Patrick's history, died and was interred in the Cathedral crypt near the remains of New York's archbishops. A few years later, Cardinal Cooke, who had been suffering silently from cancer for years, died and was laid to rest in the same crypt.

From the very start of the episcopate of John Cardinal O'Connor, the next archbishop, in 1984 it became obvious that the pulpit of St. Patrick's would be used to proclaim clearly the authentic teaching of the Catholic Church. His public profile was higher than that of any of his predecessors, and objections by those differing with Catholic teaching were frequent and vociferous through demonstrations both inside and outside the Cathedral. With rare exceptions he celebrated a solemn liturgy every Sunday and huge crowds were the norm. Prominent figures, both ecclesiastical, such as visiting cardinals, and civic, such as presidents of nations or famous entertainment figures, were in attendance. The Cardinal presided at almost constant special liturgies commemorating such events as the

• *John Cardinal O'Connor.*
Photo Credit: Chris Sheridan

• Relic of St. Patrick.
Photo Credit: John Glover

28

centennial of the Statue of Liberty; the opening of the Marian Year; the 600th anniversary of Lithuanian Christianity; the 500th anniversary of Columbus' discovery of the new world; and the 50th anniversary of the United Nations, to mention just a few.

In 1988 the Cardinal appointed Msgr. Anthony Dalla Villa to succeed Msgr. Rigney as rector. After the death of John Grady in 1990, John-Michael Caprio assumed the baton in the gallery. Mr. Caprio added three choirs to the existing one and continued the program of special religious concerts. Over several years, Msgr. Dalla Villa brought luster to every area of the Cathedral, restoring statues, sacred vessels, the baldachin, the pews and, outside, the terraces and steps. The first complete restoration of the massive bells in the north tower was undertaken at the same time. He commissioned the strikingly beautiful Christmas creche to be made in Italy and added some statuary near the west entrances.

In 1995 Pope John Paul II returned to St. Patrick's during his second visit as pope to New York. He led the Rosary at the Cathedral and celebrated Mass in Central Park for a large crowd. The hectic pace of liturgical activity continued for the next several years until the Cardinal's death in 2000.

• *Pope John Paul II, during his second visit to New York in 1995. Photo Credit: Osservatore Romano*

*• Installation of
Archbishop Edward Egan.*

In May of that same year, Edward Cardinal Egan took the reins of the Archdiocese and began a program of reorganization of the Archdiocese. In 2001 he appointed Msgr. Eugene Clark as new rector of the Cathedral. The attack on the World Trade Center the same year thrust St. Patrick's into a long period of constant memorial services as the remains of victims were slowly discovered month after tortured month. Funeral processions frequently accompanied by formations of thousands of firefighters, police officers and others tragically lined 5th Avenue in front of the Cathedral, so frequently that people came to expect the heart-rending sight. As so often in history, the consolation of prayer in time of great distress was a central part of the mission of St. Patrick's.

As healing slowly took root, liturgies often took on a happier aspect. In 2003, Dr. Jennifer Pascual became Director of Music. A Mass in celebration of the 125th anniversary of the opening of St. Patrick's was offered by Cardinal Egan in 2004. Msgr. Clark arranged the complete restoration of the Lady Chapel, its first in a century, and a new altar in honor of Polish saints was installed shortly afterwards. Msgr. Robert Ritchie was appointed St. Patrick's seventh rector in 2006. He immediately introduced for the first time a regularly scheduled Mass in Spanish for the large numbers of Hispanic visitors to the Cathedral. His regular custom of greeting

visitors at the doors and his general accessibility despite his demanding schedule is a source of amazement to many.

Cardinal Egan's great happiness was apparent at every event as he accompanied Pope Benedict XVI during his visit to New York. For the first time in history a reigning pope celebrated the Eucharist in St. Patrick's in the Spring of 2008. Early in 2009 Cardinal Egan announced his retirement and introduced his successor.

• *Pope Benedict XVI at St. Patrick's Cathedral during his papal visit in April 2008.*
Photo Credit: Osservatore Romano

• Pope Benedict XVI at St. Patrick's Cathedral during his papal visit in April 2008.
Photo Credit: Osservatore Romano

New York's ninth archbishop, Timothy M. Dolan, was installed in a grand ceremony in St. Patrick's in April 2009. Immediately, his ebullient joy and energy, evident during his frequent liturgies and other appearances, won the hearts of all those he welcomed to his cathedral, the most famous church in America.

• *Installation of Archbishop Timothy M. Dolan.*
Photo Credit: Chris Sheridan

THE EXTERIOR
OF the Cathedral

The **ARCHITECTURE**

The architect James Renwick's design for St. Patrick's combined French, German and English elements. It is likely that he was greatly influenced by the Church of Ste. Clotilde in Paris designed by F. C. Gau and recognized as a model of continental Gothic Revival architecture. The building is in the form of a Latin cross with entrances placed at Fifth Avenue and at the terminals of the transepts. The twin spires rising from octagonal base towers show similarities to the cathedrals of Cologne and Regensberg. The original plan called for an additional central tower at the crossing and massive flying buttresses to support a stone ceiling as well as five chapels in a radiating design at the east end. The only flying buttresses built are on each side of the transept entrances. After Renwick's death, Charles Mathews, a New York architect, designed the present Lady chapel and the two adjacent chapels at the east end. The Cathedral with smaller buttresses taking on the appearance of pinnacles remains incomplete to this day.

The central gable on the west front rises 156 feet and the spires reach 330 feet, making St. Patrick's the tallest building in America when they were completed in 1888. The extreme exterior length is over 400 feet and the extreme width is about 175 feet in the transepts. (Inside, the length is approximately 376 feet and the width is approximately 146 feet.) The portals on Fifth Avenue and those at the transepts originally were highly decorated with intricate cusps, gargoyles protruded from the walls of the Lady Chapel, and around the building there were many niches intended for statues. In the 1940s, because of masonry damage caused by blasting for construction in the neighborhood, it became necessary to redesign the entrances, remove the gargoyles and fill the niches with solid marble.

The Gothic style is that used between 1275 and 1400 in Europe called the geometric or decorated style. It appears especially in the elaborate tracery around the windows and, inside, in the clustered pillars and highly decorated capitals. The Lady Chapel addition reflects a 13th Century French Gothic design, more elaborate than the rest of the building. Although different varieties were used at various stages of construction, the exterior walls are built entirely of marble, as are the interior lower levels and all the columns.

Photo Credit: John Glover

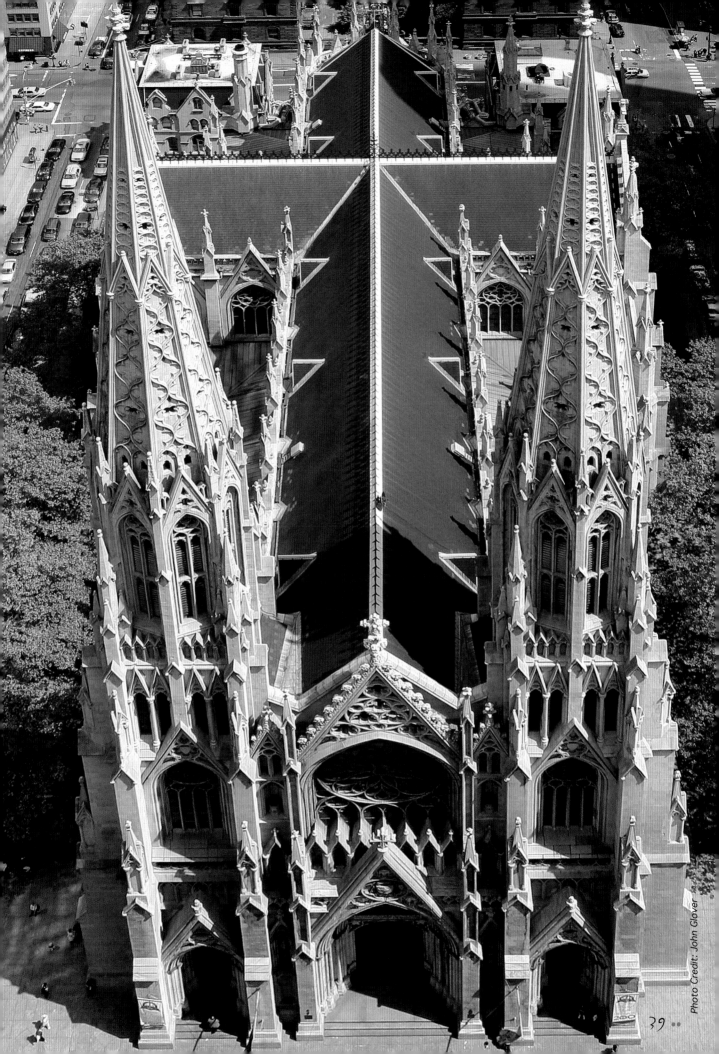

39

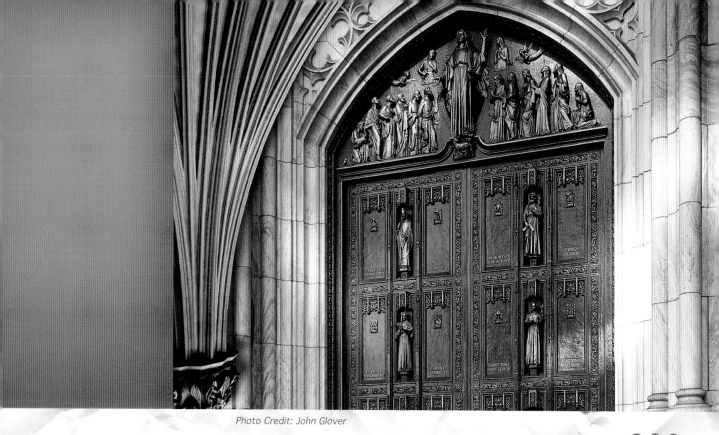

The BRONZE DOORS

Traditionally Gothic cathedrals and churches had doors made of wood whose only decoration appeared on their iron hinges. In the late 1940s, at the same time bronze doors were being made for St. Peter's Basilica and the cathedrals of Milan and Cologne, so also at St. Patrick's the work of producing new bronze doors was in progress.

Charles Maginnis of Maginnis and Walsh of Boston designed the doors. The figures on the doors were sculpted by the English artist John Angel. The Halback Company of Brooklyn, New York built the doors employing 44 men over a period of 82 weeks. The two panels of the main entrance are over 23 feet high and almost 29 feet wide with a total weight of 40,580 lbs. The doors on the tower entrances are over 29 feet high, almost 15 feet wide and weigh 16,700 lbs. at each of the four entrances. The doors are double-faced (ornamented both inside and outside). To effectuate the opening and closing of such massive heavy panels, a pivotal device using both ball bearings and roller bearings sealed in oil was installed. On the tower doors special checking devices were used.

The general motif of the designs stresses the missionary and cosmopolitan character of the Church of New York as exemplified by the figures. With each figure are displayed symbols associated with the person depicted (from left to right):

Photo Credit: John Glover

Photo Credit: John Glover

Photo Credit: John Glover

1 - **St. Joseph** is shown with a ship representing the Church and a lily, a sign of purity.

2 - **St. Isaac Jogues** is shown with a palm, a sign of martyrdom and a chalice representing his priesthood.

3 - **Blessed Kateri Tekakwitha** is shown with an eagle indicative of her native American heritage and the heraldic arms of Pope Pius XII during whose reign the doors were built.

4 - **St. Patrick** is shown with a phoenix indicating undying faith and a harp, a Celtic symbol.

5 - **St. Frances Cabrini** is shown with a dolphin representing her missionary zeal and raised hands indicating her concern for immigrants.

6 - **St. Elizabeth Seton** is shown with a rosebush, symbol of New York State and the heraldic arms of Francis Cardinal Spellman, Archbishop when the doors were built.

On the tower doors are emblems representing the unity, sanctity, universality and apostolic character of the Catholic Church, and images of a pelican, a lamp, a chalice, the scales of justice, and a crown, all symbolizing Our Lord Jesus Christ, and a heart, a symbol of Mary, the sorrowful mother.

The doors were officially dedicated when Cardinal Spellman blessed them on December 23, 1949 in time for a Christmas opening.

The BELLS

The nineteen bells in the north spire were made in Savoy, France by the Paccard Company, makers of over 80,000 bells around the world since 1796. When they arrived in New York in 1897 they were the most impressive set of bells in America, ranging in weight from 173 pounds to 6608 pounds. The bells do not swing but are equipped with clappers shaped as anchors which strike the bells. They are adorned with bas-relief sculptures of saints, Gothic ornaments and various fruits. Each bell is named and inscribed with a Latin poem.

The bells first were rung above Fifth Avenue on May 4, 1898 to mark the 25th anniversary of the episcopal ordination of Archbishop Michael Corrigan. They were silent for the next 19 months while a compressed air system with ll0-feet-long wooden rods was installed allowing them to be played from far below their location. On New Year's Eve in 1900 at midnight, strollers along Fifth Avenue listened once again to their glorious sounds. Thereafter, they have been heard regularly to the present time. They were electrified in 1952, and were completely restored in 1992.

Today the bells sound the Angelus at noon and at 6 p.m. every day, followed by the music of several hymns. The hymns are played also on Sunday mornings before the solemn Mass.

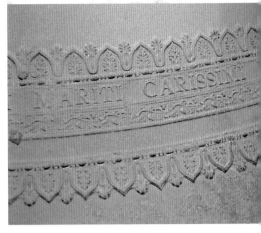

Photo Credit: John Glover

The bells with specific identifying information are:

St. Patrick	B flat	6608 lbs.
Blessed Virgin Mary	C	4625.5 lbs.
St. Joseph	D	3260 lbs.
Holy Name	E flat	2693 lbs.
St. Michael	E	2319 lbs.
St. Anne	F	1956 lbs.
St. Elizabeth	G	1357 lbs.
St. Augustine	A flat	1162.7 lbs.
St. Anthony of Padua	A	971.13 lbs.
St. Agnes	B flat	802 lbs.
St. John the Evangelist	B	667.7 lbs.
St. Bridget	C	574 lbs.
St. Francis Xavier	C sharp	476.3 lbs.
St. Peter	D	401.5 lbs.
St. Cecilia	E flat	345 lbs.
St. Helena	E	286 lbs.
St. Alphonsus Liguori	F	240.9 lbs.
St. Thomas Aquinas	F sharp	204 lbs.
St. Godfrey	G	173 lbs.

Photo Credit: John Glover

The STATUES ON THE EXTERIOR

When the Cathedral was opened in 1879, there were niches for 51 statues on the exterior facade and for twelve more in the coves of the jambs at Fifth Avenue. Only two niches received statues and almost all the rest were filled with marble in the 1940s to counter deterioration. On each side of the 5th Avenue portal are statues of the Immaculate Conception and of St. Joseph, installed in the 1890s and made in Roermond, Holland.

The 15 feet high Carrara marble statue of St. Francis of Assisi on the Cathedral terrace, previously located inside the building, was blessed by Cardinal Hayes in 1928 to commemorate the 700th anniversary of the saint's death. It is a reproduction of the statue sculpted by Dupre for the Cathedral of Assisi.

The 8 feet high copper statue of the Virgin Mary atop the Lady Chapel was blessed by Cardinal Cooke in 1978 for the Cathedral's centennial year celebrations.

Photo Credit: John Glover

Photo Credit: John Glover

THE INTERIOR

OF *the Cathedral*

The CHANCEL (SANCTUARY)

The chancel is the heart of the Cathedral, because it is here where the Holy Sacrifice of the Mass is offered. Until the mid-1980s, the high altar with its imposing baldachin (canopy) was where the Mass was celebrated before the liturgical altar was set near the front of the sanctuary. The high altar and baldachin were designed by Maginnis and Walsh of Boston and installed in 1942. The predella (platform) on which the altar rests is made of Tavernelle Italian marble. The frontal of the altar contains a decorative motif symbolizing the Church. St. Peter, the first pope, appears at the stern of a small boat (the Church) whose rudder he is guiding. The baldachin soars 57 feet above the pavement, terminating with a statuette of St. Michael the Archangel. It is made entirely of bronze and its decorative theme is the redemption of mankind. Nine statuettes facing the rear (east) represent Old Testament figures as well as St. John the Baptist, St. Peter and, at top center, Christ the Messiah. On the front (west) at the top center is a statuette of Christ the King and High Priest. Below are figures of various New Testament saints.

The liturgical altar close to the steps, designed by the Cathedral's architect James Renwick, was made in 1893 for the Holy Family chapel. It has served as the principal liturgical altar since 1985.

The marble floor has inlays of figures symbolic of Christ Our Redeemer, of the Holy Eucharist, and of the four Evangelists.. To each side are sedilia (seating) for seventy clerics. A screen in Gothic design surrounds the entire sanctuary.

The *cathedra*, or Archbishop's chair, is near the front on the left with statuettes of Sts. Peter and Paul carved on the back, together with the heraldic arms of the archbishop of New York. Adjoining the pillar near the front right is the magnificent octagonal pulpit, made in Italy in 1886 using several varieties of marble, most of which came from the same quarry from which were made the columns of the portico of the Pantheon in Rome. Statuettes of St. John the Evangelist, St. Peter, St. Patrick, St. Paul and St. Andrew adorn the corners.

Photo Credit: Patrick Danczewski

Photo Credit: Peter Mauss/Esto

Suspended from the high vaulting over the sanctuary are four ceremonial red hats, called galeros, belonging to four cardinals entombed in the crypt below the high altar. This centuries-old tradition was ended during the Second Vatican Council; therefore no hats appear for the last two New York cardinals.

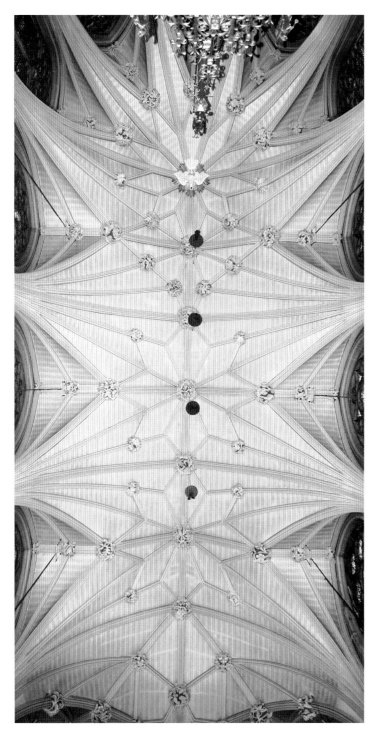

Photo Credit: Peter Mauss/Esto

Photo Credit: John Glover

Photo Credit: John Glover

The graceful communion railing separating the sanctuary from the nave is made of Tavernelle and Swiss Cipolin marbles with a bronze gate at the center. In the thirteen niches are statuettes of saintly figures devoted to the Holy Eucharist: St. Juliana; St. Clare; St. Paschal Baylon; St. Bernard of Clairvaux; St. Thomas Aquinas; St. John the Evangelist; St. Peter; St. Paul; St. Alphonsus Liguori; St. John Vianney; St. Tarsicius; Blessed Imelda; and St. Margaret Mary.

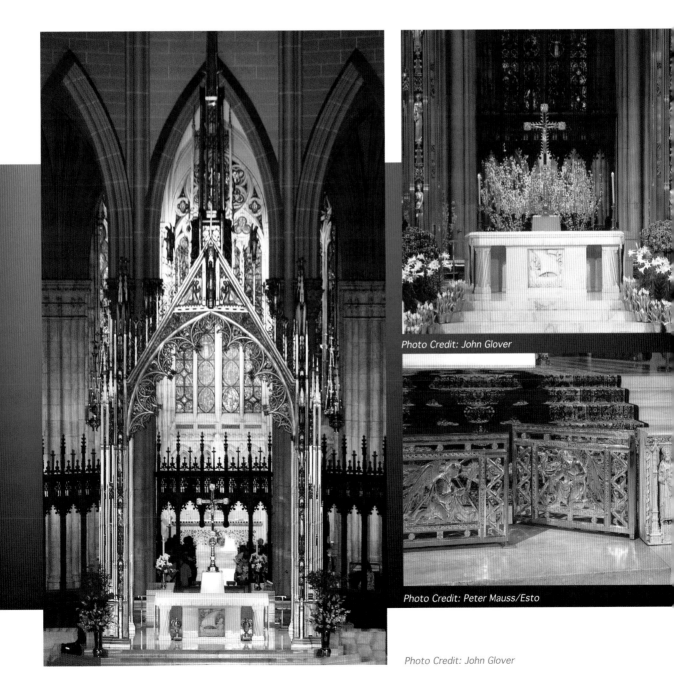

Photo Credit: John Glover

Photo Credit: Peter Mauss/Esto

Photo Credit: John Glover

The LADY CHAPEL
AND ADJOINING CHAPELS

Often called the "architectural gem" of the Cathedral, the Lady Chapel and the two adjoining chapels were an addition to Renwick's building, and constructed between 1901 and 1908 according to the 13th Century French Gothic design of Charles Mathews, a New York architect. Many who have visited Paris' Sainte Chapelle note the similarity of design between the two.

The vaulted ceiling is 56 feet high and the width is 28 feet. The entire interior including the windows was restored in recent years and the floor was replaced with new polished marble in a mosaic pattern.

The altar was built in 1942 of Tavernelle marble with a design on the frontal representing the Annunciation. Above the altar is the tabernacle which houses the sacred Hosts, the Body and Blood of Our Lord. The statue of Our Lady of New York appears with outstretched arms, a position called orans (praying) which dates to the early Church when Christians prayed in the Catacombs.

Photo Credit: John Glover

Photo Credit: John Gover

The altar of St. Elizabeth to the right of the Lady Chapel was designed by Charles Mathews, the architect, and built of Paterno marble by the Rome firm Paolo Medici and Sons (of the famous Medici family). Ideas for the panels came from sketches of Albrect Durer. Scenes represent the baptism of Our Lord by St. Elizabeth's son, St. John the Baptist and the beheading of St. John. The altar was consecrated in 1910.

Photo Credit: John Glover

Left of the Lady Chapel, the altar of St. Michael and St. Louis IX of France also was designed by Charles Mathews and was built by Tiffany and Company. Piccirilli Brothers, famous for such statues as that of Abraham Lincoln (Lincoln Memorial, Washington, D.C) and commissions by Daniel Chester French among many others in New York, were the sculptors. The altar was installed in 1908.

• *Altar of St. Michael and St. Louis IX of France .*
Photo Credit: John Glover

Photo Credit: John Glover

63

Photo Credit: Peter Mauss/Esto

The WINDOWS

The earliest windows filled with stained glass are those with large figures seen mostly at the lower levels of the walls and a few in the transept and over the sanctuary. They portray holy men and women and events from both the Old and New Testaments. They were in place when the Cathedral opened in 1879 and were made by Nicholas Lorin in Chartres and Henry Ely in Nantes, France.

Beginning in 1909 and continuing until 1934 the Lady Chapel and adjacent chapel windows were designed by Paul Vincent Woodroffe of Chipping Campden, England. His firm built ten windows and five were built by other firms in England, France and Germany. The windows portray figures associated with fifteen mysteries of the Rosary.

Photo Credit: Peter Mauss/Esto

Photo Credit: Peter Mauss/Esto

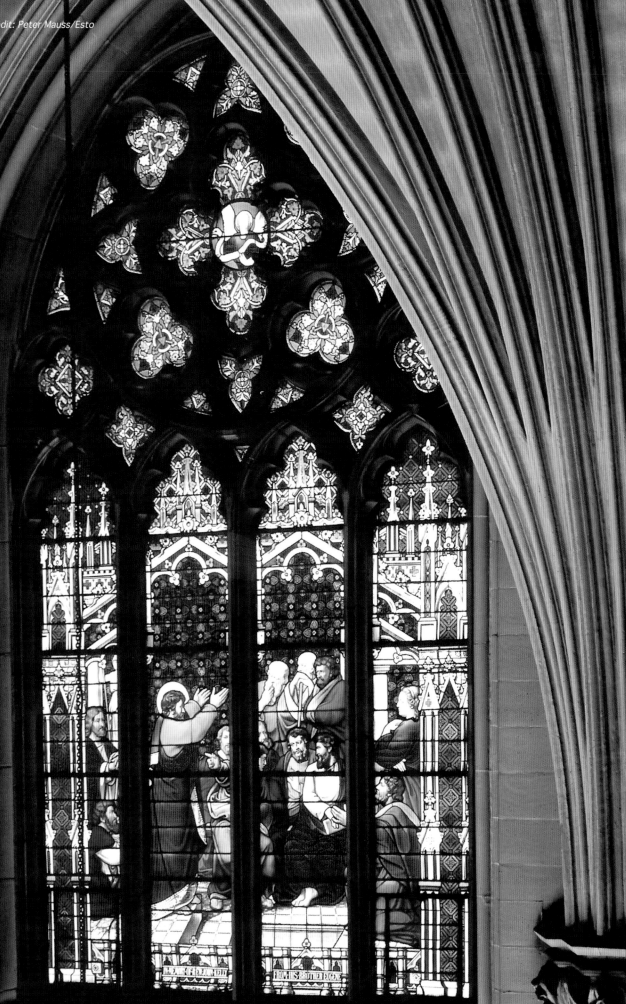

The blue-toned windows at the upper levels and the magnificent rose window over the grand organ were the work of the firm of Charles J. Connick of Boston, and installed between 1942 and 1956. The nave clerestory (upper level) windows portray various saintly persons, the windows over the apse (semicircular space around the altar) represent parables of Our Lord, and the theme of the rose window is angels whose figures represent the eight beatitudes in the petals of the rose.

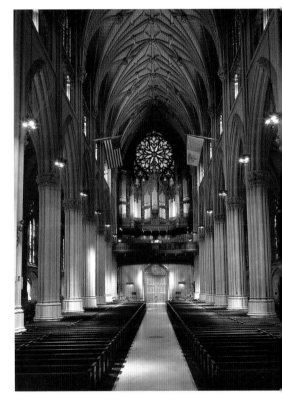

Photo Credit: David Garvey

Photo Credit: Peter Mauss/Esto

Photo Credit: Sacred Art Studio

The ALTARS AND SHRINES

1 - The Altar of St. Anthony of Padua

This 1894 Carrara and Pernici Pastello marble altar was designed by the Cathedral architect, James Renwick. The standing statue of this popular saint was recently placed in the chapel. On the Caen stone reredos (rear screen) appear the figures of St. Monica holding an open book and St. Anne with a scroll.

2 - The Altar of St. John the Evangelist

James Renwick's firm also designed this dark Siena marble altar which was built in Carrara, Italy. At the foot of the Carrara statue is an eagle, the symbol of St. John. The altar was blessed in 1894.

1

Photo Credit: John Glover

Photo Credit: John Glover

2

3 - The Shrine of St. Elizabeth Ann Seton

This modern portrayal was dedicated in 1975, following the canonization of this native saint of New York City. It was designed and sculpted by Frederick Shrady, whose work appears all over the world, including the doors of the Basilica of the Incarnation in Nazareth. Scenes on the screen are New York, Livorno, Italy where she prepared to become a Catholic, and Emmitsburg, Maryland, where she founded the American Sisters of Charity.

4 - The Altar of St. Rose of Lima

This memorial to the first native-born saint of the western hemisphere and made of various Italian marbles was dedicated in 1906. The statues of St. Catherine of Alexandria, with the wheel, an instrument used to torture her, and St. Margaret, a patroness of those suffering difficult childbirths, are on each side.

5 - The Painting of Our Lady of Guadalupe

This 18th Century painting was the work of a master, probably a disciple of Miguel Cabrera, and was presented to St. Patrick's Cathedral in 1991 by Ernesto Cardinal Corripio, Archbishop of Mexico City. The painting portrays the image which appeared miraculously on the tilma (cloak) of Juan Diego in 1531.

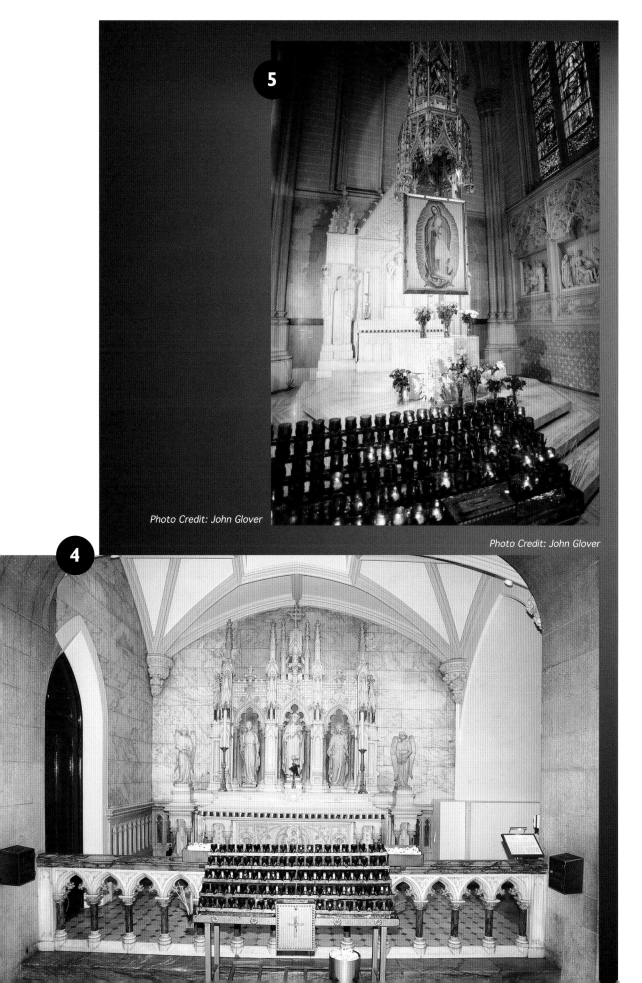

Photo Credit: John Glover

Photo Credit: John Glover

6 - The Altar of the Sacred Heart

The Gothic design of this altar by New York architect Henry Bacon, designer of the Lincoln Memorial in Washington, D. C., is unusual for him, since his specialty was classical Greek architecture. On the Carrara marble reredos is a scene of Our Lord confronting the doubting St. Thomas after the resurrection. The altar was dedicated in 1913.

7 - The Altar of St. Andrew

The Carrara marble altar bears a statue of the Apostle supporting an X-shaped cross, the instrument of his death. On the reredos appear scenes of his calling by Christ and the miracle of the loaves and fishes. The altar was consecrated in 1910.

8 - The Altar of St. Therese of Lisieux

After the canonization of St. Therese, Maginnis and Walsh designed this altar in her honor. The artist Mario Corbel built it using a wide variety of marbles in mosaic design.

The inscription records the words of St. Therese: *"I shall spend my Heaven doing good on earth."*

On the screen appear the Infant Jesus and the veil of St. Veronica. The altar was dedicated in 1928.

7

Photo Credit: John Glover

Photo Credit: John Glover

8

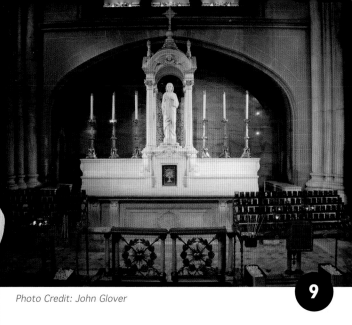

Photo Credit: John Glover

9

9 - The Altar of St. Joseph

The only Renaissance design altar in St. Patrick's was once the main altar of the Roman Catholic Orphan Asylum in the Bronx, New York. It came to St. Patrick's in 1922. The marble statue was made in the 1990s in honor of the 50th anniversary of Cardinal O'Connor's ordination to the priesthood. The altar is made of Carrara marble.

10 - The Altar of the Holy Face (St. Veronica's Veil)

The only mosaic painting in St. Patrick's appears on the reredos showing the image of Christ on the veil of St. Veronica. As on the painting from which the mosaic was copied, the eyes appear closed or turned upward or downward, depending on where one stands when observing it. The Carrara marble altar, one of James Renwick's designs, was consecrated in 1891.

11 - The Altar of Our Lady of Czestochowa

The Gothic altar surrounded by ornamental angels came to St. Patrick's from the Church of St. Thomas the Apostle in Harlem, New York, and was consecrated by Cardinal Egan in 2005. The icon of Our Lady of Czestochowa, Poland, was painted by Anna Torwird, and was blessed by Pope John Paul II. A statue of St. Stanislaus Kostka stands on the right and that of St. Casimlr on the left. On the right wall are images of St. Faustina Kowalska and St. Jadwiga, Queen of Poland; on the left are those of St. Maximilian Kolbe and St. Stanislaus, bishop and martyr.

Photo Credit: John Glover

Photo Credit: John Glover

Photo Credit: John Glover

12 - The Altar of St. John Baptist de la Salle

The Christian Brothers designed this memorial to celebrate their founder's canonization in 1900. Both the altar and the reredos employ various Italian marbles. The statue is carved from Carrara marble and on the reredos are scenes exemplifying the saint's love of charity and his care of children. On the frontal is a scene of his death. Statuettes of St. Benilde Ramançon and St. Miguel Cordero are on each side.

13 - The Altar of St. Bernard and St. Bridgid

The reredos behind the altar replicates the doorway arch of the 12th Century St. Bernard's Chapel in Millifont Abbey, Ireland. A wide variety of marbles is used on the altar and throughout the chapel. It was dedicated in 1903.

14 - The Shrine of St. Jude

This shrine honors one of the favorite saints of the Church faithful, also known as St. Jude Thaddaeus. The shrine was designed using materials from an altar in the Church of St. Thomas the Apostle in Harlem, New York. It was built in 2008 in time for the visit to the Cathedral by Pope Benedict XVI.

13

14

77

The STATIONS OF THE CROSS

The devotion of the Stations of the Cross traces to the Middle Ages. The fourteen sculptures depicting the passion and death of Our Lord are set into the walls on both sides of the transept. More than one-half life-size, they were made over a period of several years by Peter J. H. Cuypers of Holland. The first three to arrive won first prize for art at the Chicago Exhibition of 1893. The Caen stone sculptures were blessed by Archbishop Corrigan in 1900.

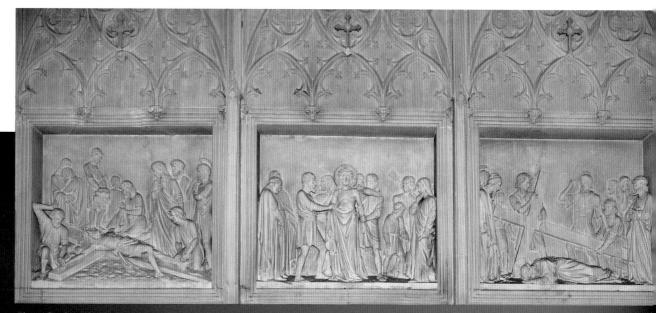

The STATUES

The Pieta

This group of the sorrowful mother Mary holding the body of her divine Son was installed at the Cathedral in 1915, nine years after it was carved by William Ordway Partridge. The Latin word *pieta* appropriately means compassion or pity.

Photo Credit: John Glover

The Doctors of the Church

The sixteen statues in niches of the transept walls are of saints noted for great learning and holiness. The doctors who are portrayed are St. Peter Canisius (not shown), St. Dominic (1) , St. Thomas Aquinas (not shown), St. Pius X (2), St. Athanasius (3) , St. Gregory Nanzianzen (4), St. Basil the Great (5) , St. John Chrysostom (6), St. Francis de Sales (7), St. Ambrose (8), St. Gregory the Great (9), St. Jerome (10), St. Anselm (not shown), St. Bernard (11), St. Bonaventure (12) and St. Alphonsus Liguori (13). Most were installed in the 1890s, but the sculptures of St. Peter Canisius and St. Pius X were added decades later. Most were made by Joseph Sibbel and John Massey Rhind.

ST. ALPHONSUS LIGO

83

St. Patrick (1)

The image of the Cathedral's patron stands on a bracket on a pier at the north side of the sanctuary. Designed by John Angel, it was erected when the high altar was built in 1943. The figure appears wearing a chasuble, the principal vestment of the Mass, and carrying a book of gospels and a shamrock.

St. Augustine (2) and St. Monica (3)

Often unnoticed because of their location high on the ambulatory walls on each side of the Lady Chapel, these marble statues of mother and son were installed in the 1920s.

St. Peter (4) and St. Paul (5)

The bronze images resting on corbels in the narthex (vestibule) near the Fifth Avenue doors were created by 80-year-old Adlai Hardin in 1983. Cardinal Cooke blessed them in March of that year.

St. Frances Xavier Cabrini (6) and St. John Bosco (7)

The relief sculpture of the Italian immigrant St. Frances Xavier Cabrini was designed by the Ferdinand Stuflesser Studio in Italy and was erected on the wall near the 51st Street entrance in 2003. Its counterpart at the 50th Street entrance, that of St. John Bosco, founder of the Salesians, was created by Elizabeth Gordon Chandler in 1998.

Pope Paul VI

At the request of Cardinal Spellman, Pope Paul VI donated this bust to commemorate his visit to the Cathedral in 1965. It was made from a casting of the original by Lello Scorzelli of Naples.

Pope John Paul II

Erected to commemorate the visit of the pope to St. Patrick's in 1979 (the pope returned for a second visit in 1995), the bust was made by Joy Buba. It was erected in 1982.

84

SAINT PETER

SAINT PAUL

The **ORGANS**

Both the grand organ in the gallery near Fifth Avenue and the chancel organ just outside the sanctuary screen were built by the Kilgen Company of St. Louis, a firm with roots in organ building tracing to 1640 in Germany. The chancel instrument was dedicated in 1928, and the grand organ in 1930 after three years of construction. The design theme of the grand organ case is angels, several of which can be seen in the beautiful wood screen designed by Robert Reiley.

The smallest pipe of the grand organ is ½ inch long and the longest is 32 feet in length and equipped with a device to produce the sound of a 64 feet-long pipe. While most of the divisions are located above the gallery, some pipes are laid lengthwise in the triforium, the mid-level area of the Cathedral below the high windows; one division, the echo organ, also is located in the triforium, but speaks out into the transepts. Both the grand organ and the chancel organ can be played individually or simultaneously from either console. The gallery organ contains 7855 pipes and the chancel organ has 1480 pipes. In addition, there are 75 chimes. The organs were completely restored over a period of several years in the 1990s.

Photo Credit: John Gover

MOST REV.
JOHN HUGHES,
FIRST ARCHBISHOP,
OF
NEW YORK.
DIED
JAN. 3RD 1864.

Photo Credit: John Glover

● ● ●

The CRYPT

Below the high altar is the burial crypt of the Archbishops of New York and several other persons deemed worthy of entombment in the Cathedral. The bronze entrance doors to the crypt can be viewed from behind the high altar at the entrance to the Lady Chapel. Following are the names of those whose remains are in the crypt: Archbishop John Hughes; John Cardinal McCloskey; Archbishop Michael Corrigan; John Cardinal Farley; Patrick Cardinal Hayes; Msgr. Michael Lavelle; Francis Cardinal Spellman; Bishop Joseph Flannelly; Archbishop Fulton Sheen; Terence Cardinal Cooke; Archbishop John Maguire; Venerable Pierre Toussaint; and John Cardinal O'Connor.

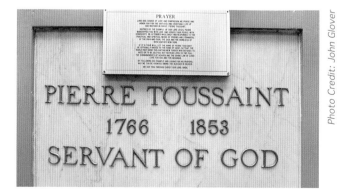

PIERRE TOUSSAINT
1766   1853
SERVANT OF GOD

Photo Credit: John Glover

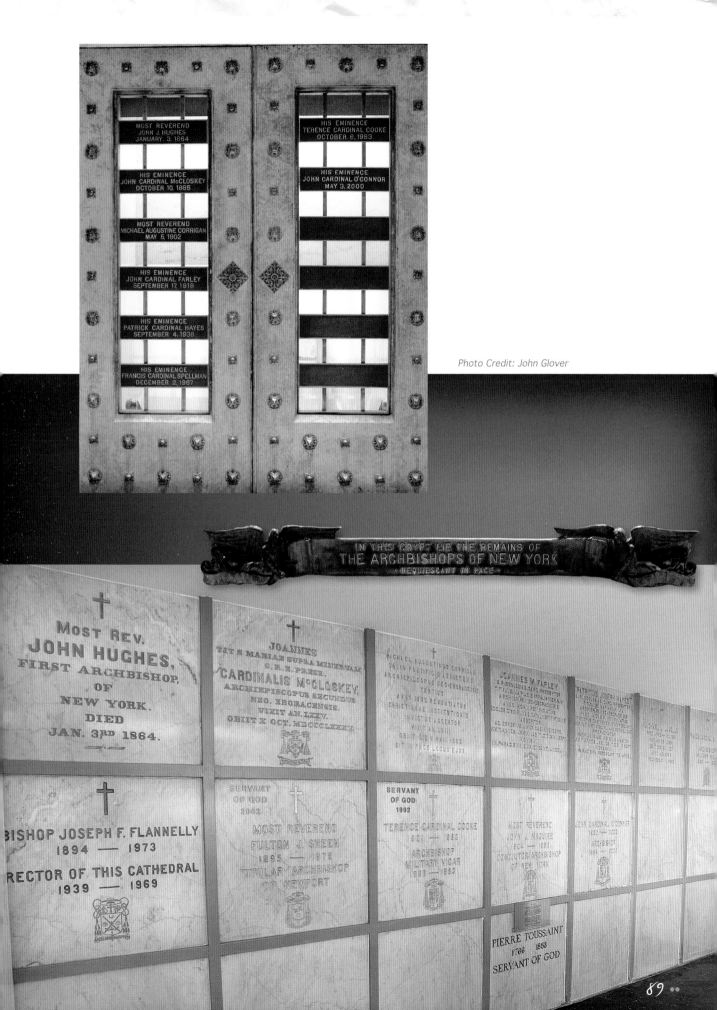

Photo Credit: John Glover

IN THIS CRYPT LIE THE REMAINS OF
THE ARCHBISHOPS OF NEW YORK
· REQUIESCANT IN PACE ·

Photo Credit: Patrick Danczewski

The **SACRISTIES**

Opposite the stairway to the crypt are stairs leading to the sacristies, rooms for vesting and storage of sacred vessels, under the Lady Chapel. The main sacristy is bordered on each side by smaller sacristies. At the rear of the main room is a small chapel originally intended for a crypt, but now furnished with an altar where private Masses are often celebrated.

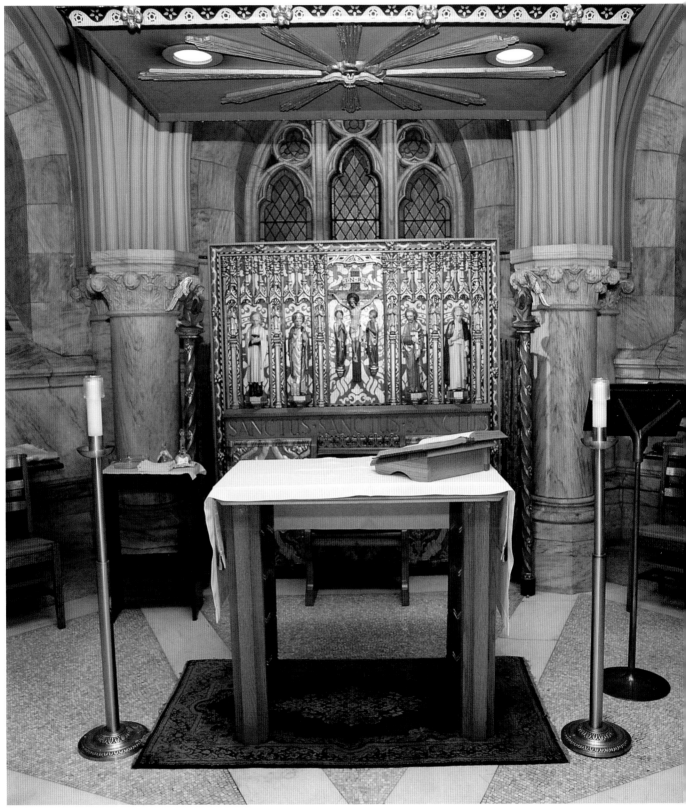

Photo Credit: John Glover

The **BAPTISTRY**

The baptistry, formerly located in a chapel near Fifth Avenue, was moved in the 1990s to where the present liturgical altar in the sanctuary had stood before. The reredos behind the font was the reredos of the liturgical altar, then called the Holy Family altar. Thus, its central panel contains a scene of the Holy Family taken from a painting of Raphael. To each side are reliefs depicting the Annunciation and the Adoration of the Magi.

The baptismal font is made of Bottocino marble. Suspended above is a gilded cover carved from oak.

The FLOOR PLAN

• • •

1 - Gift Shop and Holy Water Font
2 - Altar of Saint Anthony of Padua, Saint Ann, Saint Monica
3 - Altar of St. John the Evangelist
4 - Shrine of St. Elizabeth Ann Seton
5 - Altar of Saint Rose of Lima, Saint Catherine,
    Saint Margaret
6 - Stations of the Cross
7 - South Transept Entrance
8 - Altar of the Sacred Heart,
    Painting of Our Lady of Guadalupe
9 - Altar of St. Andrew
10 - Altar of St. Teresa of the Infant Jesus
     (The Little Flower)
11 - Archbishop's Sacristy
12 - Pieta
13 - Altar of St. Elizabeth
14 - Entrance to Crypt and Sacristies
15 - Altar of St. Michael and St. Louis
16 - Ushers' Office
17 - Altar of St. Joseph
18 - Chancel Organ
19 - Baptistry
20 - Liturgical Altar
21 - High Altar and Baldachin
22 - Pulpit
23 - Statue of Saint Patrick
24 - Archbishop's Throne
25 - Cardinals' Hats (above)
26 - North Transept Entrance
27 - Altar of the Holy Face (Saint Veronica's Veil)
28 - Shrine of Our Lady of Czestochowa
29 - Altar of Saint John Baptist de la Salle
30 - Altar of Saints Brigid and Bernard
31 - Altar of Saint Jude
32 - Statue of Saint Paul
33 - Bas relief of Saint John Bosco
34 - Bronze Doors
35 - Statue of Saint Peter
36 - Bas relief of Saint Frances Cabrini
37 - Information Desk

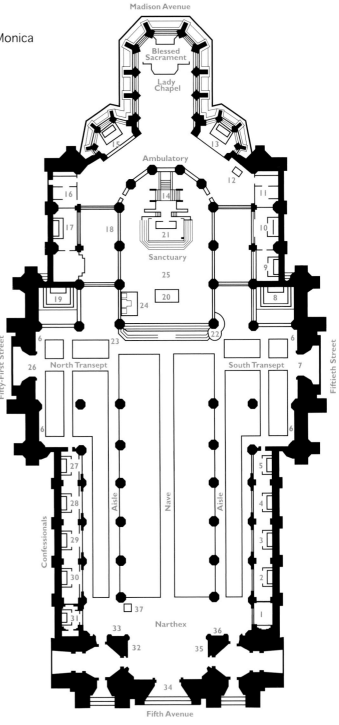

95 ••